The Developing

Artist

**AUDIO
INCLUDED**

PIANO LITERATURE BOOK 4

ORIGINAL KEYBOARD CLASSICS

REVISED EDITION

Late Intermediate

Compiled and edited by

Nancy and Randall Faber

Production: Frank and Gail Hackinson
Production Coordinator: Philip Groeber
Cover: Terpstra Design, San Francisco
Engraving: Tempo Music Press, Inc.

FABER
PIANO ADVENTURES®
3042 Creek Drive
Ann Arbor, Michigan 48108

2

TABLE OF CONTENTS

THE PERIODS OF MUSIC HISTORY

BAROQUE: 1600 – 1750

The term "Baroque" is used to describe the highly decorative style of art and architecture of the 17th century. It was an era of grandeur—of glittering royal courts in Europe, elaborate clothing, and wigs on men.

Music of the Baroque period was often highly ornate. Melodic lines were ornamented with trills or other embellishments. The Baroque period is also known for its use of counterpoint. Counterpoint ("note against note") is the technique of interweaving two or more melodic lines that imitate and support each other.

For most of this period the harpsichord, clavichord, and organ were the keyboard instruments used. The piano was not invented until about 1730.

CLASSICAL: 1750 – circa 1830

The Classical period was a time of two major revolutions: the American Revolution in 1776, and the French Revolution in 1789. Though the revolutions marked the rise of the middle class, men of the aristocracy still wore wigs and lace on formal occasions. Women curtsied and men bowed as they politely danced the minuet.

Composers of the Classical period preferred music that was charming and entertaining. They sought a return to simplicity and to what is "natural." Music of the period was elegant and melodic, avoiding counterpoint and using ornaments sparingly. "Taste" was very important, with purity and clarity as key elements of composition.

Haydn, Mozart, and Beethoven were the major composers of the Classical period. (Much of Beethoven's late work, however, ushered in the Romantic period.) These composers from Vienna were the creators of the piano sonata, the string quartet, and the orchestral symphony.

The keyboard instrument of this period was an early version of the piano called the fortepiano. The fortepiano was a rather delicate instrument with a light, clear tone. By the time Beethoven was an adult, however, the piano had increased in size, strength, and keyboard range. Now called the pianoforte, the instrument's power and dramatic capabilities made it an ideal instrument for the emerging Romantic period.

Romantic: circa 1830–1910

The Romantic period in music, art, and literature coincided with the rapid growth of industrial manufacturing in Europe and America, and with the westward expansion of the United States. It was also the time of America's Civil War and Queen Victoria's reign over the British Empire.

Music became openly emotional, and personal expression became more important than "taste" or pleasing an audience. With imagination and inspiration, composers often based their music on legends, folk songs, and fanciful tales of romance.

Orchestras increased in size and symphonic works became long and dramatic. The concerto (a composition for soloist and orchestra) became a work of technical display, designed to showcase a virtuoso soloist.

The 19th century may be considered the high point for piano music. The solo piano recital was popular in public concerts and in the private homes of the wealthy. With shadings of touch and pedal, the piano offered intense personal expression. Rubato—a flexible "give and take" in the rhythm—contributed to the emotional power of music and became a hallmark of the Romantic style.

Contemporary: circa 1900 – present

This century has been called the Age of Extremes. It has been dominated by two world wars (1914–1918 and 1939–1945), the Great Depression, and the breakup of both the British and Soviet Empires. It has also been a time of extraordinary technological advance. New forms of communication and travel staggered the imagination: telephone, radio, phonograph, motion pictures, television, the computer, automobiles, aircraft, and even spaceships!

Percussive effects, changing time signatures, abrupt rhythms, and dramatic contrasts are characteristic of modern music. Dissonance and extreme chromatic writing led to atonality (music having no key).

Experimentation has been a powerful force in 20th century music composition. Improvisation and such novel effects as plucking strings inside the piano have also added to the excitement and variety of contemporary piano music.

Minuet in D Minor

Johann Heinrich Buttstedt
(1666–1727)

Intrada

Christoph Graupner
(1683–1760)

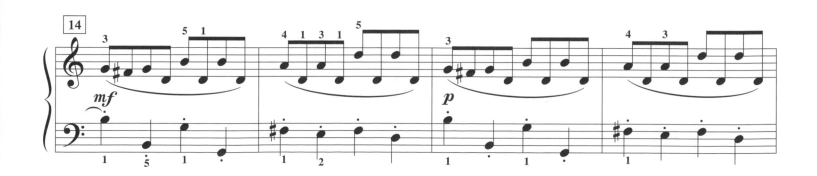

Bourrée in E Minor
(from *Suite in E Minor for Lute*)

Johann Sebastian Bach
(1685–1750)

Moderato

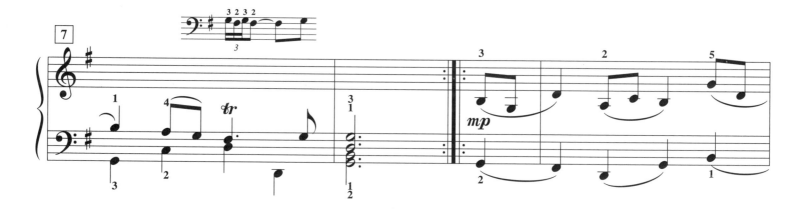

*The quarter notes should be played slightly detached.

Folia

Alessandro Scarlatti
(1660–1725)

Andantino

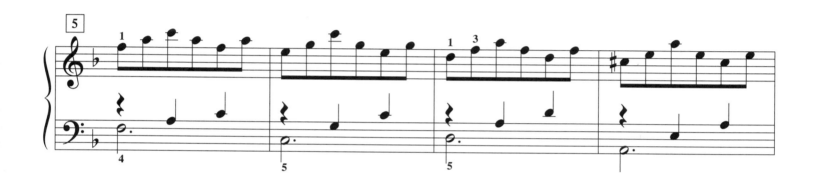

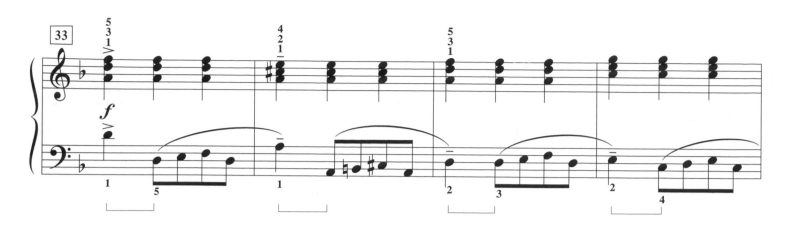

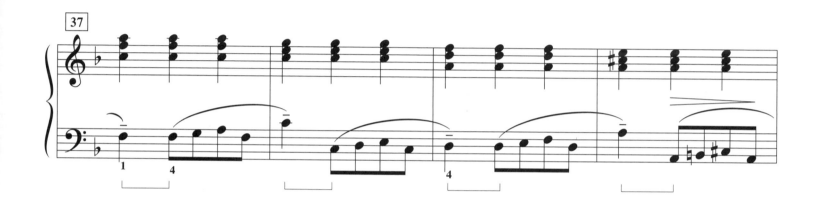

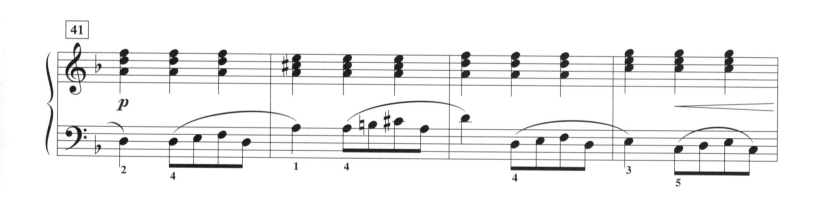

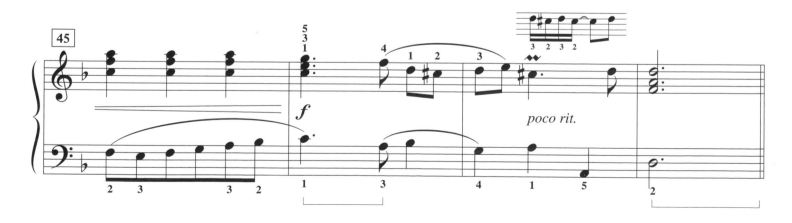

Presto
(from *Sonata in C Minor*)

Giovanni Battista Pescetti
(1704–1766)

Little Prelude in C Major
(BWV 939)

Johann Sebastian Bach
(1685–1750)

Little Prelude in F Major
(from the *Notebook for Wilhelm Friedemann Bach*) (BWV 927)

Johann Sebastian Bach
(1685–1750)

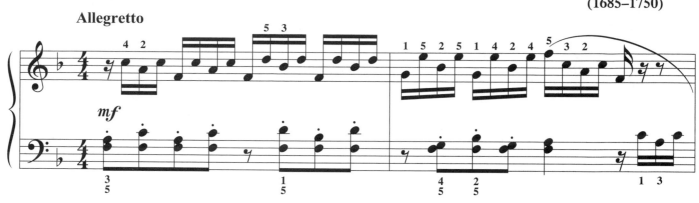

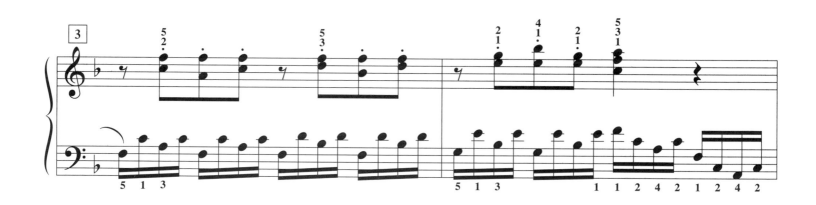

Musette in G Major
(Gavotte II from *English Suite* No. 3, BWV 808)

Johann Sebastian Bach
(1685–1750)

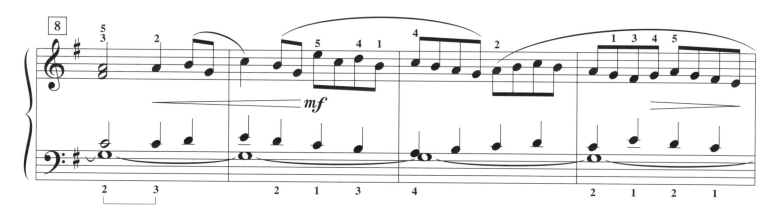

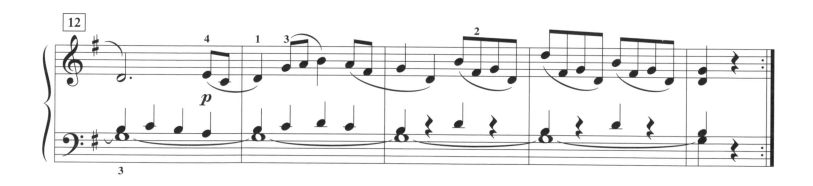

Prelude in C Major
(No. 1 from *The Well-Tempered Clavier*, Book I)

Johann Sebastian Bach
(1685–1750)

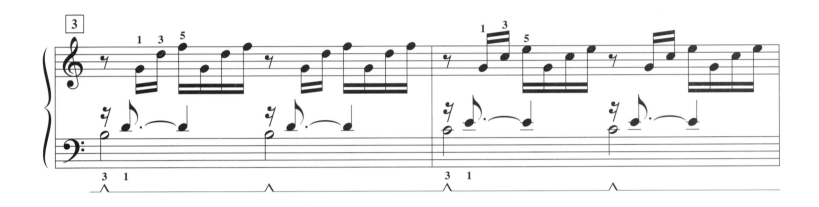

ped. simile

CLASSICAL
1750 – circa 1830

Solfeggietto

Carl Philipp Emanuel Bach
(1714–1788)

Allegro vivace

optional

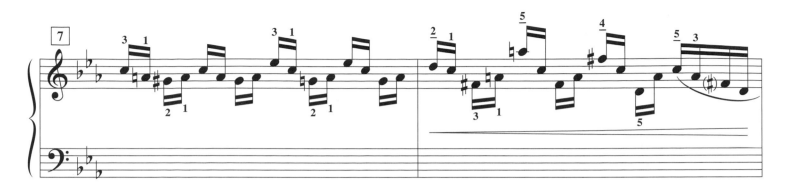

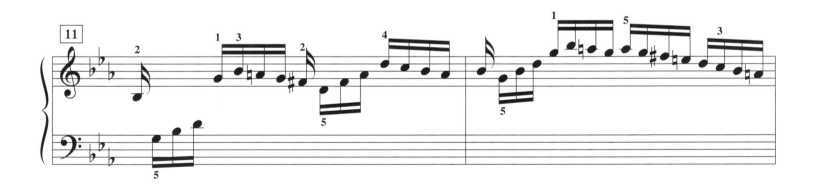

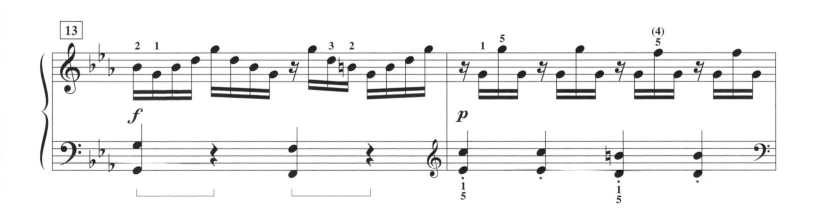

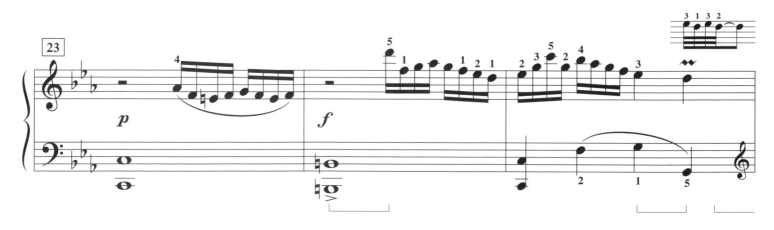

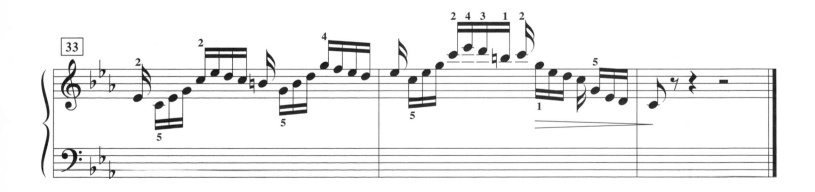

FF1282

Minuet in G Major
(WoO 10, No. 2)

Ludwig van Beethoven
(1770–1827)

a) Detach the octave leaps.

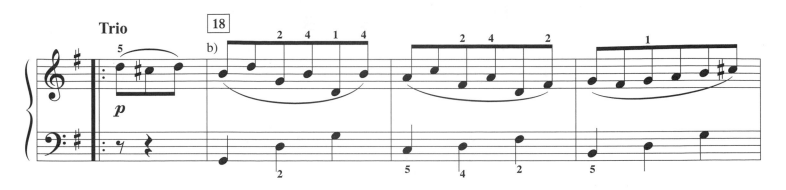

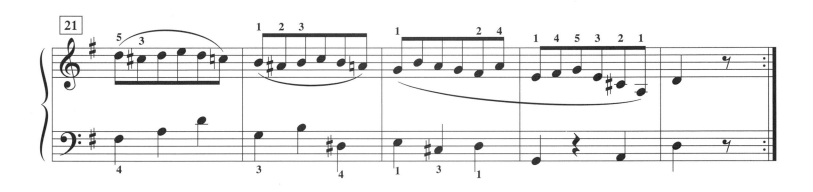

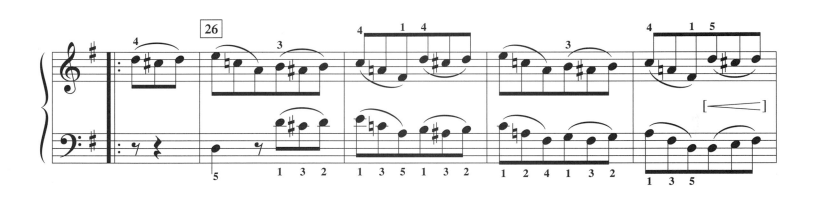

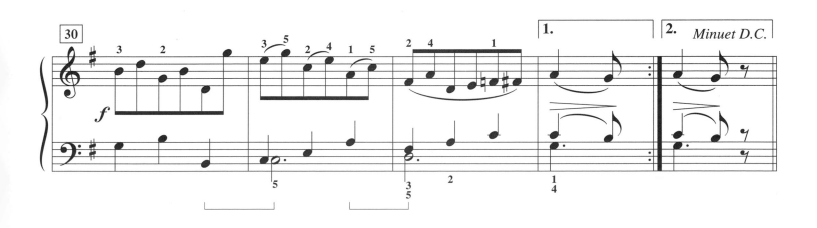

b) For the repeats, vary the articulation. Example:

Allegro in A Major

Wilhelm Friedemann Bach
(1710–1784)

*The long pedal is editorial. The passage may also be played detached, without pedal.

Sonatina in C Major
(Opus 55, No. 1)

Friedrich Kuhlau
(1786–1832)

Sonatina in G Major
(Opus 36, No. 2)

Muzio Clementi
(1752–1832)

FF1282

43

FF1282

44

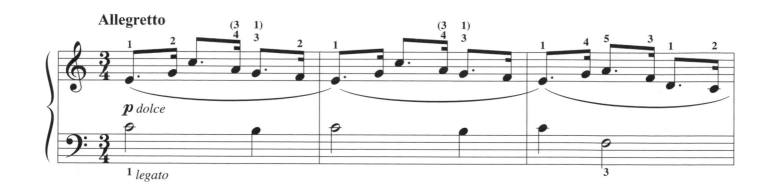

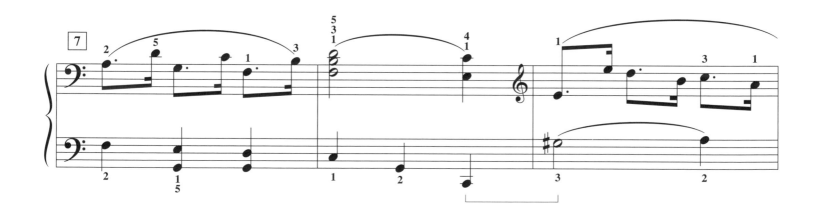

Allegro

48

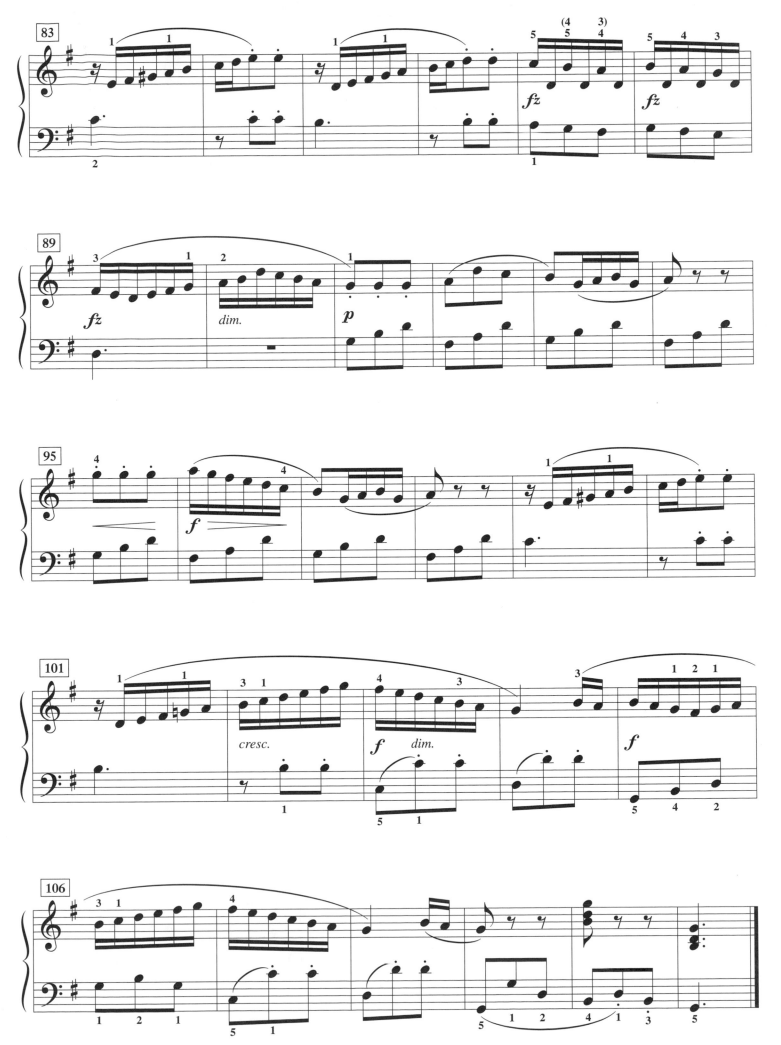

Sonatina in A Minor

Jiri Antonin Benda
(1722–1795)

51

FF1282

Für Elise

Klavierstück
(Piano piece "for Elise")

Ludwig van Beethoven
(1770–1827)

Poco moto (a little motion)

*This E can be taken with the R.H. thumb.

54

56

FF1282

Concerto in C

Franz Joseph Haydn
(1732–1809)

*or simpler:

Menuet

68

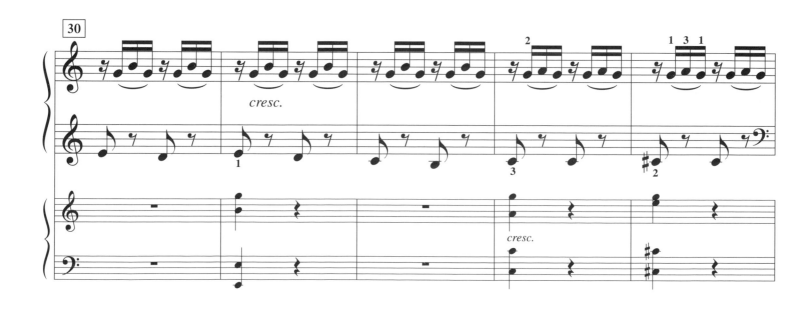

Romantic
circa 1830–1910

Miniature

Cornelius Gurlitt
(1820–1901)

Allegretto con moto

Scherzo in D Minor

Cornelius Gurlitt
(1820–1901)

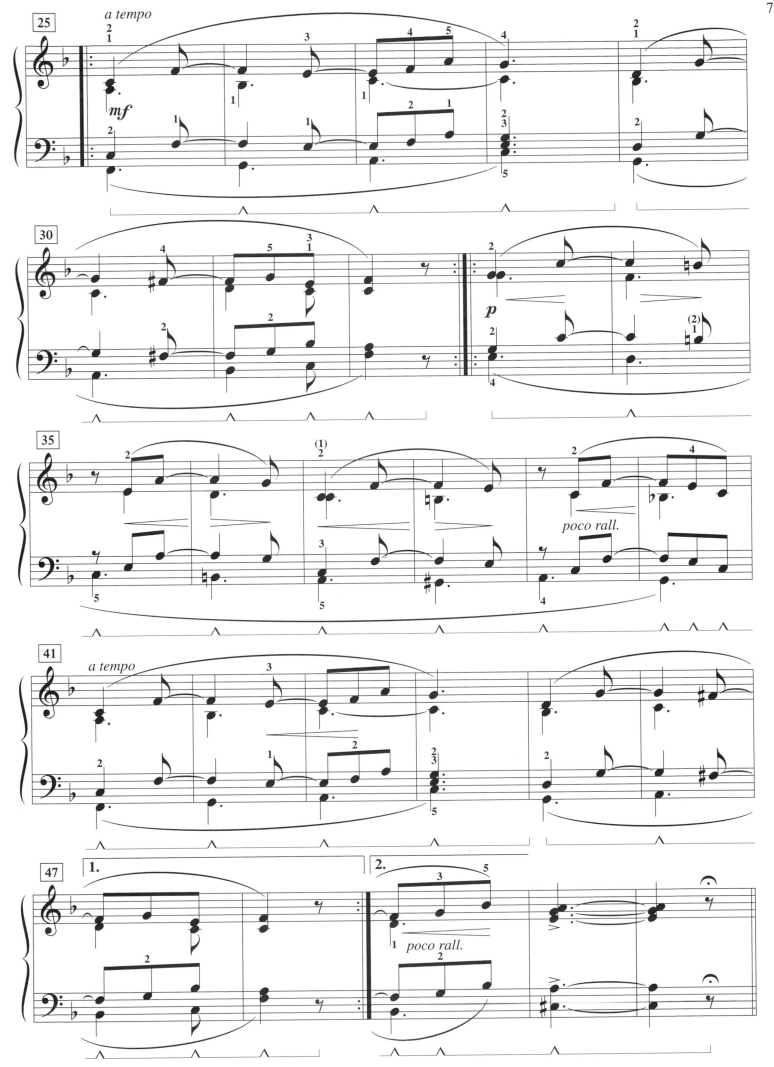

78

Sweet Dream
(from *Album for the Young*, Opus 39, No. 21)

Peter Ilyich Tchaikovsky
(1840–1893)

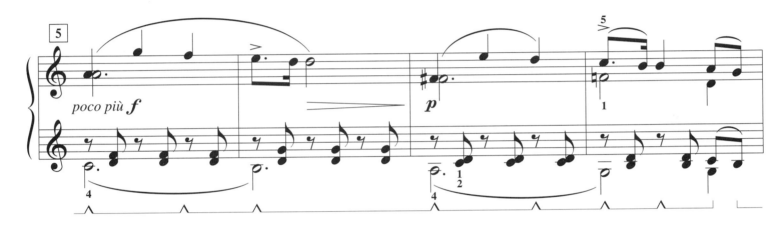

Watchman's Song
(Opus 12, No. 3)

Edvard Grieg
(1843–1907)

Molto andante e semplice

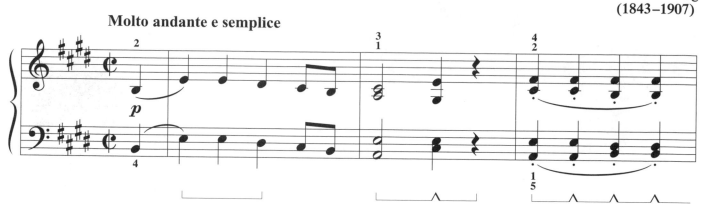

ped. simile

84

Intermezzo
(Spirits of the Night)

Sailor's Song
(Opus 68, No. 1)

Edvard Grieg
(1843–1907)

Allegro vivace e marcato

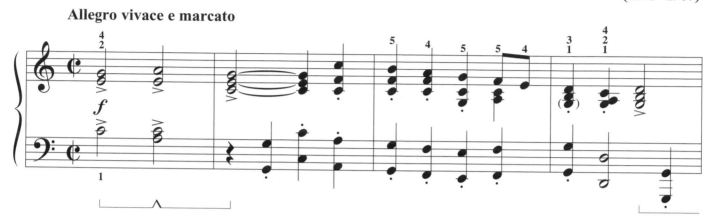

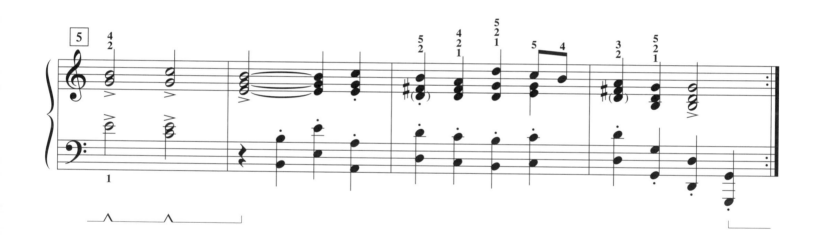

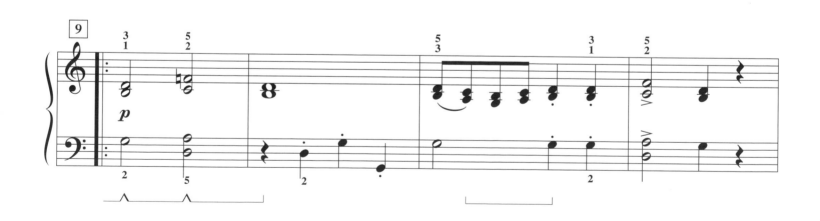

Canoeing
(Opus 119, No. 3)

Amy Marcy Cheney Beach
(1867–1944)

Tranquillo e sempre legato

melody marcato

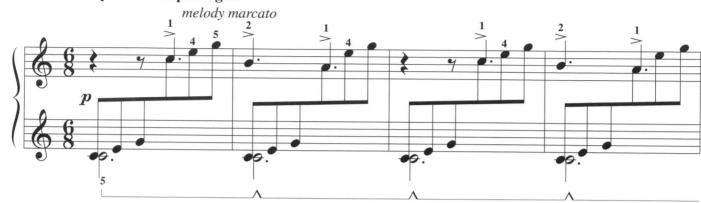

L'Orage
The Storm (Opus 109, No. 13)

Johann Friedrich Burgmüller
(1806–1874)

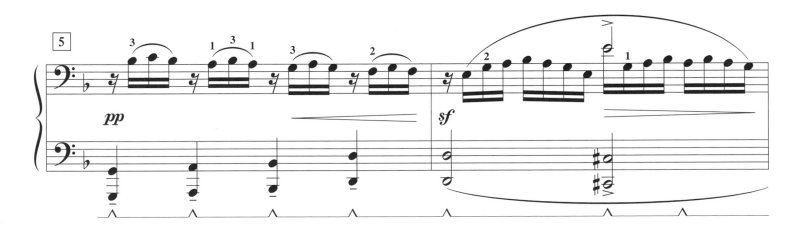

FF1282

Waltz in A Minor
(Opus posthumous*)

Frédéric Chopin
(1810–1849)

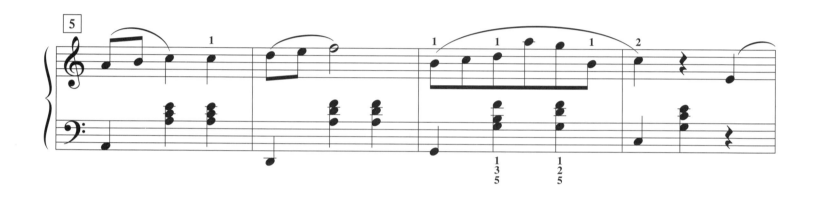

*published after the composer's death

Mazurka in F Major
(Opus 68, No. 3)

Frédéric Chopin
(1810–1849)

Allegro ma non troppo

Note: **Ped.** indicates the composer's marking.

⌐_____⌐ indicates editorial suggestions.

Prelude in B Minor
(Opus 28, No. 6)

Frédéric Chopin
(1810–1849)

Lento assai

sotto voce

Prelude in E Minor
(Opus 28, No. 4)

Frédéric Chopin
(1810–1849)

Adagio and Furiant
(from *Sonatina in D Minor*)

Zdeněk Fibich
(1850–1900)

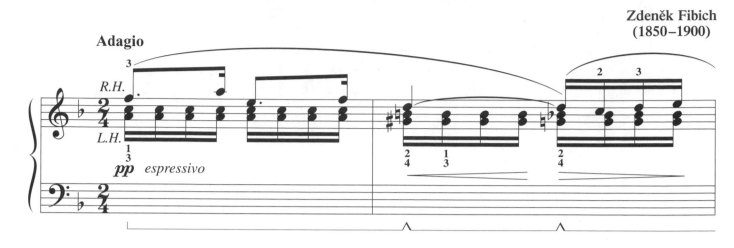

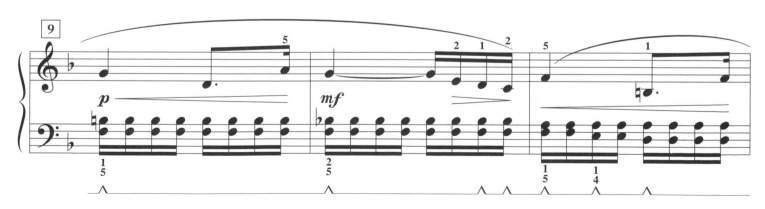

105

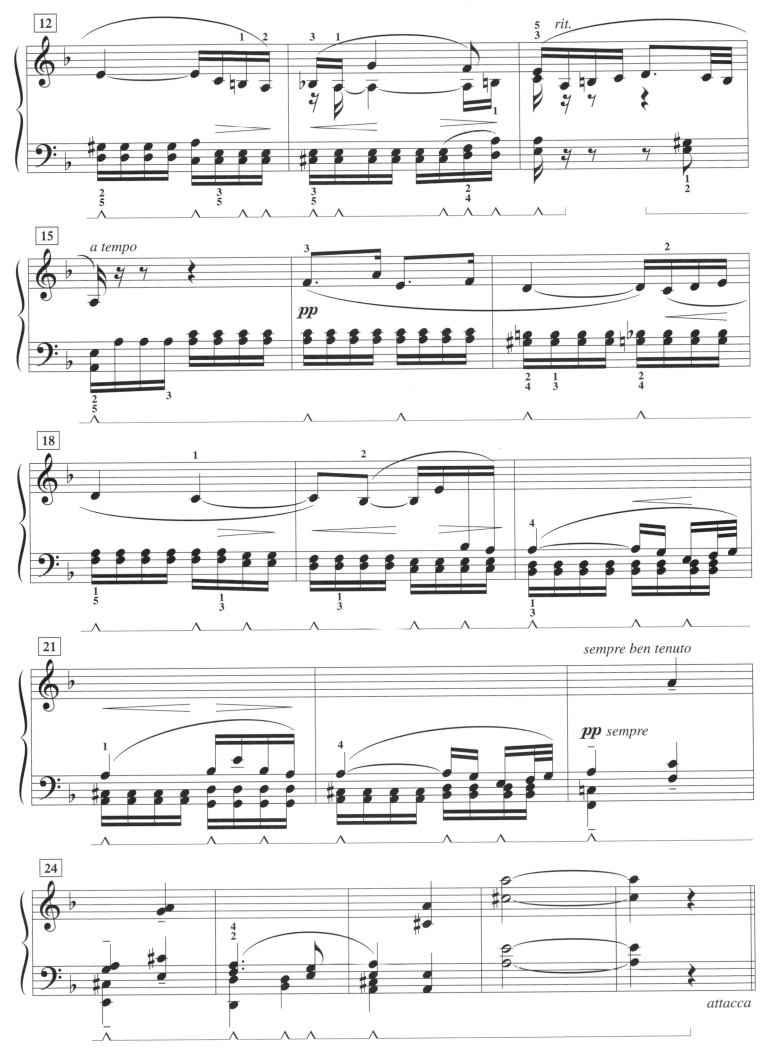

FF1282

Furiant

*The A may be held in the pedal through mm. 51–58.

108

Contemporary
circa 1900 – present

Dance with a Bell

Vladimir Rebikov
(1866–1920)

Allegretto

In the Forest
(Opus 51, No. 4)

Vladimir Rebikov
(1866–1920)

Distant Sierras

(from *Sagebrush Country*, No. 4)

George Frederick McKay
(1899–1970)

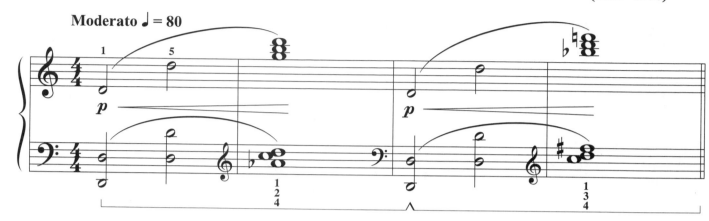

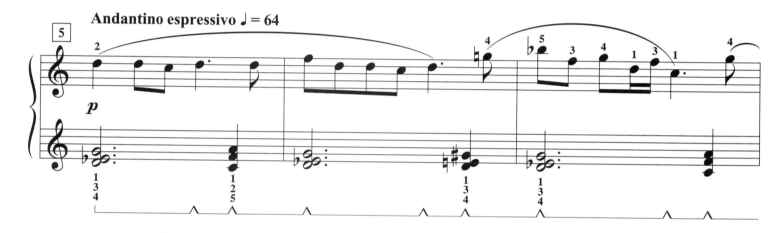

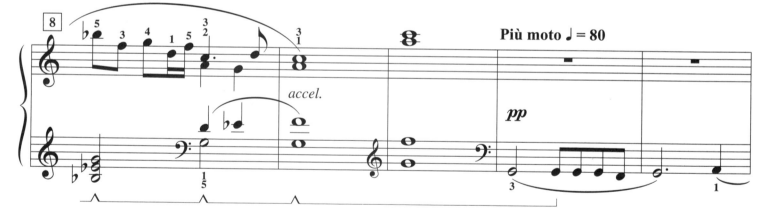

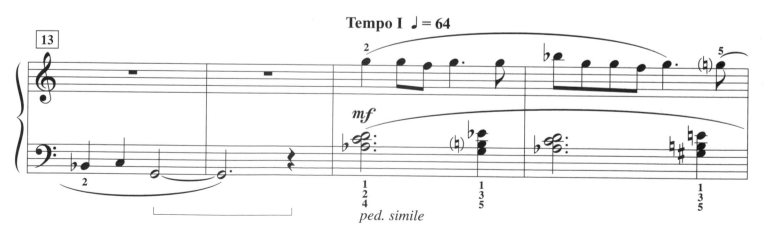

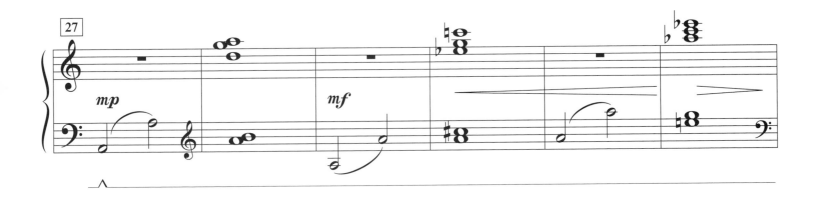

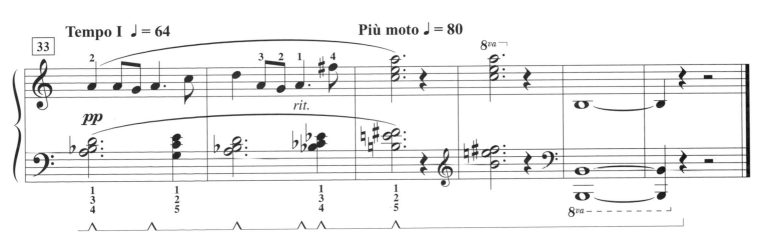

Bronco Bill

George Frederick McKay
(1899–1970)

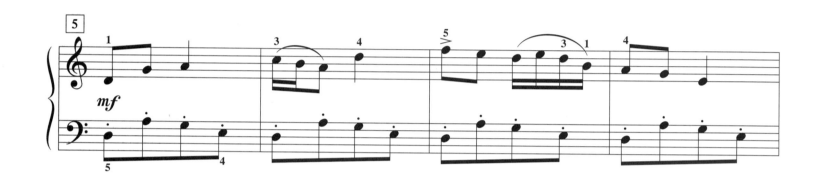

FF1282

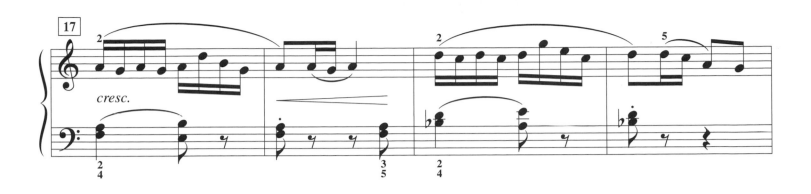

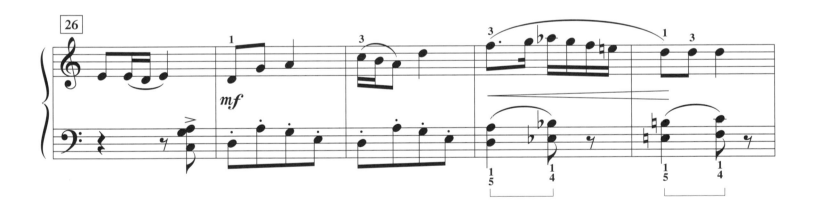

Ride of Pegasus

Nancy Faber
(1955–)

Winter Painting

Nancy Faber
(1955–)

121

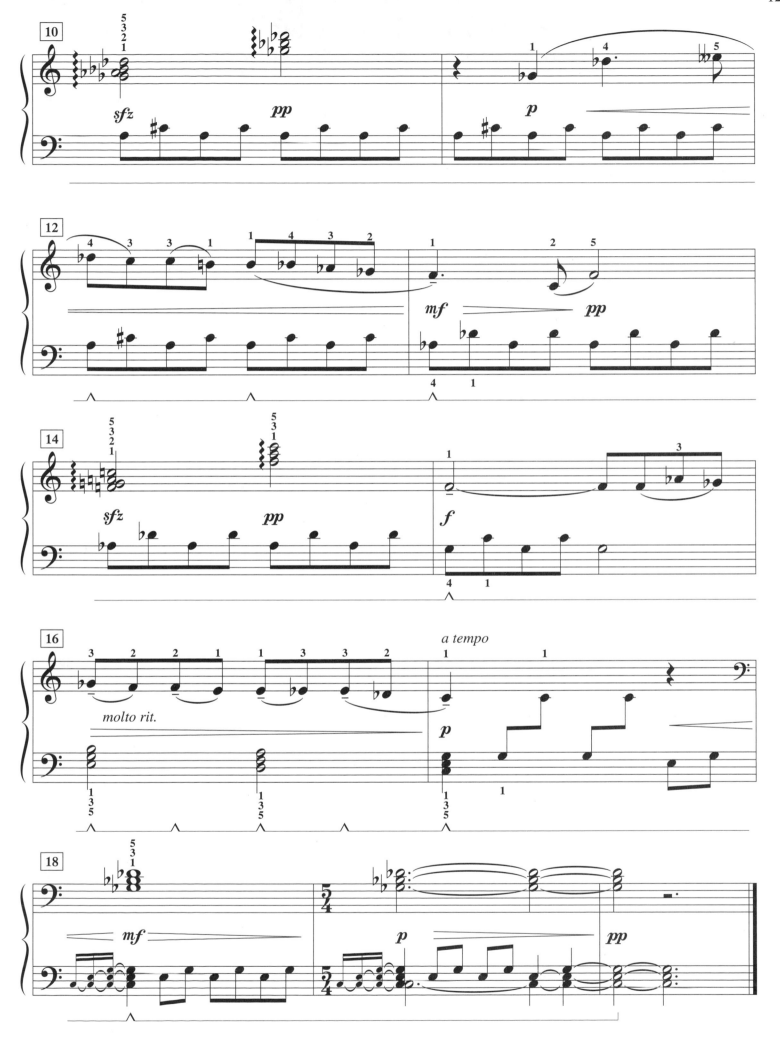

FF1282

Giant Purple Butterflies
(from *A Trip Through the Rain Forest*)

Wynn-Anne Rossi
(1956–)

Flowing, expressive (♩ = 116-144)

gradually lift pedal

ALPHABETICAL INDEX OF TITLES

DICTIONARY OF MUSICAL TERMS

DYNAMIC MARKS

pp	*p*	*mp*	*mf*	*f*	*ff*
pianissimo	*piano*	*mezzo piano*	*mezzo forte*	*forte*	*fortissimo*
very soft	soft	moderately soft	moderately loud	loud	very loud

crescendo (cresc.)

Play gradually louder.

diminuendo (dim.) or decrescendo (decresc.)

Play gradually softer.

TEMPO MARKS

Adagio	*Andante*	*Moderato*	*Allegretto*	*Allegro*	*Vivace*
slowly	"walking speed" (slower than *Moderato*)	moderate tempo	rather fast	fast and lively	very fast

SIGN	TERM	DEFINITION
	a tempo	Return to the beginning tempo (speed).
accel.	*accelerando*	Gradually play faster.
¢	*alla breve*	Cut time. Short for ²⁄₂ time signature. The half note gets the beat. (Two half note beats per measure.)
	allegro moderato	Moderately fast.
	andantino	A tempo that is a bit faster than *andante*.
	anima/animato	Animated/animatedly; played with life.
	assai	Much. For example, *allegro assai* means "quite fast."
	attacca	Begin the next movement without a break.
BWV	**Bach-Werke-Verzeichnis**	The catalog of the complete works of Johann Sebastian Bach.
	ben	With; using.
	bourrée	A 27th century French dance in duple meter.
	cantabile	Singing.
	con	With.
	concerto	A piece for solo instrument and orchestra.
	D.C. al Fine	*Da Capo al Fine*. Return to the beginning and play until *Fine* (end).
	dolce	Sweetly.
	e	And (Italian). For example, *cresc. e rit.*
espr.	*espressivo*	Expressively.
⌢	*fermata*	Hold this note longer than usual.
	folia	An early Portuguese dance form that provides the basis for variations.
	furiant	A fiery Bohemian dance in ³⁄₄ meter, with shifting accents.
	gavotte	An old French dance in ⁴⁄₄ time, beginning with two upbeats. The gavotte is more lively than the minuet.
	intermezzo	A light piece to be played between acts of a play or opera. (Or, a piece of this character.)
	intrada	An opening piece of a festive character.
	largo	Very slowly.
	legato	Smoothly, connected.
	leggiero	With a light touch.
	lento	Slowly. Slower than *adagio*.
	loco	In the range written. (Follows an *ottava* mark.)
	lunga	Long (Italian). Wait as long as you wish.
	ma	But.

	ma non troppo	But not too fast.
	maggiore	Major.
	marcato	Marked; each note well-articulated.
	mazurka	A Polish folk dance in $\frac{3}{4}$ time.
	minore	Minor.
	minuet	A stately dance in $\frac{3}{4}$ time.
	misterioso	Mysteriously.
	molto	Very. For example, *molto rit.* means to make a big *ritard*.
⁛	**mordent**	A Baroque ornament that embellishes the principal note by "trilling" with its lower neighbor.
	moto	Motion.
	Notebook for Wilhelm Friedemann Bach	A collection of pieces by J.S. Bach used for teaching his son Wilhelm Friedemann and his other children.
Op.	**opus**	Work. A composer's compositions are often arranged in sequence, with each work given an *opus* number. Several pieces may be included in a single opus. Ex.: Op. 3, No. 1; Op. 3, No. 2, etc.
8va‒ ⌐	*ottava*	Play one octave higher than written. When 8va ‒ ⌐ is below the staff, play one octave lower.
	più	More. For example, *più cresc.* means more crescendo.
	poco	A little.
	poco a poco	Little by little.
	prelude	A short instrumental piece, often rather free in style.
	presto	Very fast.
rall.	*rallentando*	Gradually slow down. Same as *ritardando*.
rit.	*ritardando*	Gradually slow down.
riten.	*ritenuto*	Slow down the tempo (immediately, not gradually).
	scherzo	A fast, vigorous piece or movement in $\frac{3}{4}$ time.
	semplice	Simple. To be played simply, straightforwardly.
	sempre	Always. For example, *sempre staccato* means to continue playing staccato.
sfz or *sf* or *fz*	*sforzando*	A sudden, strong accent.
sim.	*simile*	Similarly. Continue in the same way. (Same pedaling, same use of staccato, etc.)
	smorzando	Dying away. (Get softer.)
	sonatina	A little sonata.
	sopra	Above; as in left hand above the right hand.
	sostenuto	With a sustaining tone. Suggests a slightly slower tempo and a rich *legato*.
	sotto voce	Literally, "under the voice"; very soft, subdued dynamic.
♩	*staccato*	Play *staccato* notes detached, disconnected.
	stretto	Chopin uses the term to indicate forward motion; a slightly pushed tempo.
sub.	*subito*	Suddenly. For example, *subito piano* means suddenly soft.
	tempo	The speed of the music.
♩	**tenuto mark**	Hold this note for its full value. Stress the note by pressing gently into the key.
tr or ∿	**trill**	A quick repetition of the principal note with the note above it. (The number and speed of the repetitions depend on the music.)
	trio	A piece for three instruments; or a section of a piece with three voices.
	vivo	With life; lively.
	waltz	A popular 19th century dance in $\frac{3}{4}$ time.

AUDIO TRACK INDEX